And the Land Dreams Darkly

Poems by Steve Gerson

Spartan Press

Spartan Press

Kansas City, Missouri

spartanpress.com

Spartan
Press

Acknowledgments:

The author would like to thank the editors of the following
publications in which some of these poems first appeared
(in one form or another):

"Alone Together;" *Howler*, "A truck in snow;" *Zoetic
Press,* "After Thought;" *Coffin Bell,* "And the morning sun
trailed her bus in shadows;" *CafeLit,* "At Midnight;" *South
Florida Poetry Journal,* "Beneath the soil;" *In Parentheses,*
"Black Stones;" *Panoplyzine,* "Breathless;" *Wingless Dreamer,*
"Contours;" *The Big Bend Literary Magazine,* "Dad's Boots;"
Vermilion, "Empty;" *Panoplyzine,* "End;" *The Bookends Review,*
"I Call Him Rusty;" *The Big Bend Literary Magazine,* "Llano
Estacado;" *The Dead Mule School of Southern Literature,* "Love/
Loveless;" *The Bookends Review,* "Love Sounds Like;" *Mantis
Poetry,* "Meditations on Bee Watching;" *In Parentheses,* "Only
geese fly in straight lines;" *Untenured,* "Pale Green and
Garnet;" *NiftyLit,* "Planting in Dry Land;" *The Gasconade
Review,* "Poetry, the land, the road: a triptych;" *Vermilion,*
"Posted;" *Panoplyzine,* "Progress;" *Snapdragon,* "Prophesies;"
CafeLit, "Rougarou Midnight;" *Cotton Xenomorph,* "Scent of
Rain;" *The Big Bend Literary Magazine,* "Sepia;" *Quibble,* "Shell;"
Leon Literature, "So much depends;" *Vermilion,* "Spring as
Self Portrait;" *The Decadent Review,* "Sunset Diorama;" *The
Big Bend Literary Magazine,* "Sunshine enters like a hesitant
guest;" *CafeLit,* "The Echo between Passing Hills;" *Strong
Beasts,* "Them;" *New Note Poetry,* "Winter as Self Portrait;"
The Decadent Review

Table of Contents:

Chapter 1: Searching

Chapter 2: Passages

Chapter 3: Love and Loss

This chapbook travels the plains and prairies from the Llano Estacado of West Texas through the Flint Hills and flatlands of Kansas, the Platte River valley in Nebraska, to the harsh terrain of the Dakotas.

And the Land Dreams Darkly is divided into three chapters: Chapter 1, Searching; Chapter 2, Passages; and Chapter 3, Love and Loss.

The book has an arc, from positive to negative, something akin to the seasonal gyre of life on the plains, from the hope and green of spring and summer to the chill and ice of fall and winter.

And the Land Dreams Darkly traces the lives of those of us who live, love, and experience loss on the prairies, as the land looms in dark dreams.

To Sharon, for whom all my poems are written.

Birdsong Quartet

1.

Bird song. Bird flight. These
are you, as soft and gentle
as cloudless air.

2.

Blithe movement. Joyful
aerials to heights. You
raise my horizons.

3.

Two birds on a line,
musical notes. Your treble
to my base. Our song.

4.

Birds dot the sky like
messages, singing our
consonance.

Chapter 1: Searching

Poetry, the land, the road: a triptych

1.

Poetry, like the land, like the road, seeks distance.
Ride a highway through high plains, air as thin as
dissonance, the centerline painted askew in similes.
Clouds silently see a road wrought with words.

2.

A poem wends visions labyrinthian beyond
the curvature of the earth, the highway
undulating in the blinding hum of heat.
Even roadside trees tremble for the taste of sound.

3.

The sun parts the clouds in slanted rhyme,
dappling the road with shadowed pen strokes.
Written in lightning ellipses, a poem roils in
storm song, thunder touching paper.

The Moment

Fall days when the orchards are full Ozark Gold LuraRed
Granny Smith near the Weston bend of the Missouri
and pumpkins gourds a Halloween ghost inside the
barn become haunted house for the kids and we'd sit
on benches to drink our cider eat pork ribs with sides
of salad that mom had picked that morning from the
garden carrots lettuce snap peas and maybe Jim would
play us a tune his fingers bowing a store-bought fiddle
and night would come on soft in the east like a coverlet
drawn the air cooling and fireflies illuminating our land
and we'd glow in the harmony of family knowing good
times are followed sometimes by you just never know

Planting in Dry Land

I'll grow me dry beans since what the hell else
is gonna sprout in a hundred and two

and the desert is dreaming about rain long gone
pinto and navy, kidney and black,

so down I dig, deeper than most,
to ferret what moisture hides under rocks,

and jam them bean shells at least thumb deep
and use my canteen to drench them some

before covering them up with dry dust mulch,
wipe my sweat on my chambray sleeve,

put my gimme hat atop my head,
squint at the sun glaring through cloudless skies,

then trudge back to my barn to sip on a brew,
and wait.

And the morning sun trailed her bus in shadows

When she turned 18, it was time, she thought, to find it, a road, a path, somewhere, anywhere. So, she packed her duds in an overnight, stole what cash she could scrounge from her ma's secret hiding place in the shoebox behind the Christmas wrapping paper on top of the outdated *People* magazines growing mold in their attic, and set off—5:00 am, on foot, toward the Greyhound bus depot on 2nd and Main, trying to leave the house before her mom woke for a morning shift at the Sip and Suds convenience store slash laundromat slash icehouse. Her dad was long gone, having left for a one-night bender, fifteen years ago. Walking through the still-dark streets with only dogs wailing loneliness, moths swirling around lampposts anxiously, she laid low in the depot's restroom, then boarded the 7:15 am bus to Amarillo, heading north, her line of destiny, she thought, traveling the direct path toward a trade, maybe wealth, or at least something akin to $7 an hour plus tips, love, who knows, even marriage. Sitting on the bus's back row, alone, on a brown vinyl seat cracked like drought-hard clay, she wrote a note to no one in her diary, decorated with rainbows and hand-penciled hearts. She was charting a life, the morning sun trailing her bus in shadows.

Scent of Rain

agave prongs pleading
mesquite branches wrenched
their gnarled pod-like fingers
yearning wither blistered
red ants derisive of succulents dried
into hollowed bones wind whistling
as flute moans through the arroyo

but in the distance of prairie distance between
Palo Duro to Prairie Dog Town and shimmering
heat against skyless clouds under shadowless noons
a gray cumulus rises builds piles like canyon peaks
the flattening base sending shafts of slanted hope
diaphanous sheets backlit and a breeze suffused
with sand promises a scent of rain

Contours

He worked with oak, madrone, and mesquite,
wood that resisted his plane and saw,
desert-hard wood, withered and wrought,

wood that had strangled through rocky soil
with branches that whined for a scent of rain,
to make his chairs, tables, and toys,

live-edged in burnished blemishes,
wood with creaks, crooks, and cracks.
He wanted wood that lived the land,

mesquite that roiled in Chisos silhouettes,
madrone whose inner bark shined
Chihuahuan red, oak that endured

drought and deluge, his saw breaking teeth
on resin hard knots, his T-square hopeless
against cantankerous wood.

So he beat his knuckles raw, hammered his thumbs,
cursed when splinters punctured his skin,
and planed and polished the wood to shine,

awl-carved and turned the woods' wending bends,
to showcase their depth, color, and courage
against the terrors of land, wind, dust, and freeze,

to make of what he'd been given
from the land he loved, to touch
with his hands the contours of time.

Shell

In my youth, we traveled the back roads from Sedalia to Cottonwood Falls, Tulsa to Omaha, the roads coiling like a nest of snakes, we four staying each night in a fleabag motel, paying 31 cents per gallon at one-pump stations, our '57 Olds, 264,000 miles on the odometer, sucking gas like a four-pack-a-day smoker, the junk's hood hooked to the front bumper with baling wire, a proverb painted on the rear window from Matthew's "thrown into the furnace of fire," the four of us eating at drive-ins, greasy chicken or fried burgers: "don't spill none of that soda on the upholstery," dad would threaten, "just remember oysters don't spit out pearls all the time, we don't got money to burn" as he'd drive from one revival meeting to the next, preaching the gospel: "oh lord on high, we got sinners among us who better fear, cuz' hellfire's around the bend," but around our bend was the red dust and dirt of another road, another tent, another night in another sway-backed motel with its parking lot of broken cement, weeds sprouting through the cracks like dreams awakening in a nightmare, and him shouting damnation gospel, his voice the groan of an undertow, the pull of riptide: Revelation 19 ("thrown them alive into the lake of fire which burns with brimstone") or Thessalonians 1 ("These will pay the penalty of eternal destruction") and now, it all in a rearview mirror, my eyes squinting in the glare, my throat scorched from swallowing his perdition, my soul as empty as a closed roadside diner along a bypassed road, I think about how cement is made from crushed shells.

I call him Rusty

I was jogging through mesquite and pine
looming above rock soil baked
hard in the August sun when I heard
it the patter of clicks like metronome
snicks clawed nails gaining on me
and I feared a coyote or riled wild boar
angry at my invasion me a man out of place
in this land remote from town where
only buzzards felt at home in their dead sky
no breeze the stillness of thermals
so I took a backward glance and readied
myself for defense against whatever
desert denizen stalked but stopped
and welcomed instead a lop-eared tagless
mutt the color of sand more red than tan
more rust than dust his hide burr-tangled
and knotted in dirt and as I slowed he
loped and skid-slid to a stop his eyes
rheumy his tongue a slop and he sat
and waited for a ruffled pat a pull
on his ear before I set off on my jog
renewed my partner now a companion dog
still stuck to me like a tick on blood

Then/Now

We retired from the city
to our cabin retreat
cleaning our past for the future

"That feels good George to rid
ourselves like wadding up calendar
pages and tossing them chaff

to the wind" and we moved on the 9th
opening windows to let our hearts
pulse new life George saying "can't wait

Barb to sit on that porch under them trees
and hear mockingbirds whistle trills"
and the sky was blue for three days

then we got the news flash "seek
shelter instability" and the blue sky
turned gray with cloud striations

the shape of raptor talons clawing
when wind shears shifted and our
trees shook above the cabin the sound

of a rasp filing our roof like teeth
and trees shattered leaves swirling
like pages torn from tomorrow

Black Stones

Roberto and Jesus left the scorched
fields of Saltillo with six pesos,
a pocket of cornmeal, and a liter Coke

bottle of water to travel toward Piedras
Negras at the Texas border near Eagle Pass.
They trod like coyote through Mexico,

through the Chihuahuan Desert, through
saguaro thorns and dry gulch bones, threading
ICE and armed home guard, cresting buttes

under vulture eyes, climbing barbed wire fences
slicing their skin, entangling their hopes.
They sought family in Dodge City,

700 miles north through Eldorado,
beaten by sun, harried by wind,
where the brothers could work the meat plants,

travel east to Wichita to cut hay, then north to
Kansas City for apple picking, migrating with
the seasons, seeking labor wanted.

They patched their clothes with baling string,
quenched their thirst with rainbows, walked the
black stones in search of America.

Dad's Boots

My dad's Nocona cowboy boots
vermin-skinned steel-toed
lie in my basement beneath
six cans of used paint mostly
black a child's broken toy
lost when a forgotten niece
visited dried flower arrangements
from a failed Thanksgiving
petals dropping like panicked
dreams the boot shafts tightly
stitched adorned with predatory
red tail hawks perched
each talon pinioning prey
on faded cacti the spines
exclamation points shrieking
heels rundown and dirt-caked
a barbed wire scar bisecting
the left instep like the serrated edge
of a thunderstorm the boots the color
of bad blood

Llano Estacado

I could look behind to see nothing
I could look forward and see no more
nothingness calling me like fasting hunger
as I drove my pickup beyond the county line

the veil of city haze opening to infinity the
borderless plains of the Southwest between
Amarillo and Abilene absence enveloping sound
succumbing to space dust plumes replacing people

in the miles of distance that unencumbered land creates
a crow separated from its murder first a black hollow like
a fault line on the periphery neared on the empty air
each flap of its shimmering blackness bringing the caw's

croak until within range it settled on a migrant mesquite
like a message dead-eyed staring a rebuke for trespass
feinting with a crooked neck thrusting dominance in the
domain of empty land without the safety of strangers numb

in routine compliant in numbers emptiness scalded like
breathing arid air the Llano Estacado where the wisp of line
between plain and sky snakes circumnavigating
    surrounded
by distant sibilance the hum of expectation the moan of
    despair

Progress

I saw him hollow, my father's substance emptied once returning from the war to inherit our mom-and-pop corner store from his father-in-law, selling lettuce but not arugula, mushrooms but not shitake, giving credit to neighbors in need.

"Pay me later when you can, no problem," waving to friends from the store door, knowing everyone's first name and their kids' favorite ice cream flavors, how Aunt Rose was feeling after her fall and whether John had gotten his new job.

But the superstore moved in like a thunderstorm, progress, selling pear-infused balsamic, selling more stock cheaper, 24/7, without credit, without recognition of neighbors, undercutting his margins and community like blood draining bruised platelets.

And our corner store sank as a patient amputated into a hospital bed. He then waved at friends as they drove past the door like an open casket, he a widower at a wake, while he sold off perishables, then canned goods at discounts, finally equipment—shelving, meat saws, and grinders, until the store hollowed, became skeletal, the fossilized floor scarred where feet once walked, marred from phantom pain.

I watched him evaporate, our small-town store excised in progress.

End

He started baling hay at 5:00 that morning, then he and
his boys branded cows at 8:00, breakfast missed, again.
He'd heft the heifers and throw them down, while a son
hit the cow with the hot iron, The Bar Double B, the
hair sizzling, smelling like what his Sunday school teacher
must have meant by fires of hell, "mephitis" she called it,
in her prim voice, all nose and lavender perfume.

After tending the herd, the latter part of the day was
spent stringing barbed wire between the post oaks.
No lunch, again. Only one torn thumbnail on his left
hand; only one burn on his right palm. Not bad for a
day's work. But the sons were off to the city for "real
work," they said, in a bank or insurance job. He faced
the setting sun, gray clouds heavy on the horizon, the
weather uncertain as the farm's future. He rested one
heel on the fence, his Nocona boot tip scuffed and torn,
his Llano Stetson low, a shadow on his face.

And he thought of generations past, his generation
passing like farm loans due, unpaid.

Rougarou Midnight

I poled my shallow draft through the swamp, Spanish moss covered, each wisp draping on me in a mummy's cloth, caressing my skin in spider webs. A chill wind slithered through the humidity like a cottonmouth late in October.

I didn't want to be there, damned algae-clogged waters, turgid in mud sludge, midnight owls screeching, crocs thrashing in the underbrush, heard though unseen. But me and Marie needed to eat, and my job at the Piggly Wiggly sacking groceries wasn't paying enough to keep us in red beans much less rice.

So here I was, poling, ready to gig toads or seine some crawdads. I'd set a trawl line to hook a cat or snapper—anything. When your belly's as empty as a leaky oil drum and your credit's as holey as Palm Sunday, it don't matter whatever. My back aching from the pole, I tied up to a cypress stump lichen-slick, pulled out my pack of Pall Malls, lit up, and set to rest a spell, the full moon glaring from behind sodden clouds.

Then I felt a tug on the trawl line, just a shiver at first like a cold snap, so I threw my smoke in the water, hearing the flame hiss like a swarm of mosquitoes. I wrapped the line three times around my left hand and drew in some slack with my right. There it was again, a tug, like a gator mouthing my bait for taste before grabbing hold. Another tug, this one harder, then another, so I pulled tight to set my hook.

Up rose a presence, a specter, more nightmare than swamp denizen. I'd say a head, but that wouldn't do it justice. I'd say a body, but that wouldn't tell the tale neither. What I saw in the night's gloom of shadow and fear was something from one of my grandma's ghoul stories, those she told us kids at night to scare the bejesus out of us when we was acting bad. Emerging from the dank water, its body covered in marsh reeds dangling like tomb rot, its head with boar horns, its gaping maw tooth-jagged, and eyes red like a storm brewing in the Gulf was a Rougarou, a beast from Cajun lore and moonshine drink.

And he was reeling me in. I'd set the lure, but I'd become the bait.

I could smell his swamp breath of musk and decay. I could hear his teeth gnashing, clicking like nails hammered into a coffin. I could feel my body submerging into the monster's lair.

I'd like to tell you that I shared this story with Marie, with my unborn kids years later, with my grandkids around a campfire with the sweetness of marshmallows.

Can't do it. I was gone, my body never found. Searchers sought a trace—my bones maybe, my gear from the boat. But all that remained in the swamp where I had fished was what one swamper said seemed to sound like a wail in the wind, a cry within the cypress. I had become another Rougarou midnight.

Empty

The cabin slumped behind a tree break of oak limbs
shattered by heavy snow. Wind-burred slats lay

on the ground, weed choked. The cabin once nestled
next to a barn storing hay from a field now fallow,

a silo listing windward, a windmill rusted silent, blades
missing, its water trough empty. The land was empty

too as if chirring crickets quieted, soaring birds sought
sustenance elsewhere, and sibilant mice scurried from

the farm's failure, debts incurred, debts not paid. The farm's
emptiness echoed like a dry well, in the soundlessness
　　of loss.

At Midnight

At midnight, she decided.

He'd come home late, again. Saying, "no more, Babe, I promise. It won't happen, again," just like he'd said last week, the week before, last month, every damn month.

"Trust me, Hon. I mean it," crossing his heart, like a 5-year-old having been caught taking an extra cookie from his mom's sideboard. Like a 10-year-old caught smoking behind the barn. Like a 15-year-old, when I'd bet he crossed his heart as the sheriff arrested him for killing the neighbor's kitten, wringing its neck, then hammering the cat to Mrs. Smith's red oak with four, tenpenny nails.

No more is right she thought, as he stumbled to bed, scratching his ass, kicking his lizard skin boots off.

She was through believing his pleas for forgiveness. She was through imbibing his lies, swallowing them like she'd seen him chug a can of beer, belch, wipe his mouth on his left sleeve, then crush the can. Like he'd crushed her, her trust, her hope.

As she heard him snore, all nasal and congested from his twice-broken nose, she started gathering. She picked up little Bobby, 3 years 6 months, from his thrift store crib, placing him under her right arm while she grabbed his blue teddy with her left. She'd get what she could later.

Then, she and Bobby opened his double-wide's screen door to the driveway, trying to shush the door's bleating creaks, and quietly unlocked her Honda Civic's passenger side to hook him into his car seat. She rushed to the driver's side, jumped in, turned the key, and they were off, probably to her sister Rosalee, two cities to the south.

Her Civic had 257 thousand miles on it, hard driven, maintenance rarely kept up, typical for him, she thought. "Why tend to something when it's easier to just let it die, a price to be paid later, like all his debts," mumbling silently to herself.

She'd left the trailer, though she had wanted to tell him to get the hell out. But that wouldn't have worked. He always said, yelled more like it, when they fought over his drinking, "you don't like it, git gone, girl. This here's my house, my money's paying for it, my sweat been poured while you fetch for the little one." She had no way to counter his diatribe, his height as he loomed over her, his fists, if the drink was alive in him like a nest of coiled cottonmouth snakes.

The car's rear bumper was rusted into cancerous boils from the sea air prevalent around Port Lavaca, southwest of Houston. The bumper dangled about a foot, held on by twists of baling wire. When she drove, the bumper bounced off the road, whining in the two-part dissonance of her life: potholes clanking like punches thrown, corrosion screeching, metal against metal.

As she drove, looking once into the rearview mirror, the dawn turned an angry red against the gray sky.

Chapter 2: Passages

Passages

The gyre turns
Snow blind whiteout
Ice chill shattering
And from the depth a bud
Breaks sod and greens
To brown withered in heat
The streets mirage shimmer
And leaves color to fall
The gyre turns

So Much Depends

Our kitchen's checkerboard
tablecloth awaits
the passion of
strawberries and radishes
watermelon and tomatoes
soon to be piled into
the wheelbarrow
resting against our barn's
eastern wall while
one robin warms its
ruffled breast in the
February sunrise

Working the Mississippi Mills

I'd cross the Mississippi to work the mills,
the tool shed mossed from morning mists
risen as the river steamed, and see the child
beside the man, remembering the walk I'd
walked before, he and I. His lunch pail swung
against his pants, his grimed hand grabbing mine,

we two awash in pastels cast, the eastern sun,
a dappled stream, rusting in reflection.
"Look them furnaces, son. They draw the fire
and belch the flame, they smelt the ore and bloom
the slabs, billets drawn from scrap, to build the
layers that reach the sky." I'd look up at his words

and see my future in his present, one day I the man
next to my child, and cross the bridge to work the mills.

Painting Smoke

my easel set on the Missouri banks
tripod legs biting river clay

my canvas blank inviting paint
like sky awaiting clouds

I'd layer smoke from billowing stacks
to brush the sky with wisps of gray

flecks of crow in murderous flight
then wash the river's turgid flow

in dark pastels from an eastern sun
a steam rising from waters warm

against the cool of night to dawn
and feather the mill with moss grown green

across the bridge and trestled iron
rusting in reflection of dungarees

footpaths and ash boots singed by smelt
flaming furnaces blooming slag

the painting dark draws fire from pits
and chars the canvas with metal mists

Spring as Self Portrait

As Spring. Into the plains, south of Abilene, north of
Wichita, Kansas prairieland, where May's rain streams like
wreathed smiles and lark song flies in dappled skies,
    tallgrass wends

with prairie smoke, sweetbriar, clover, and blazing star.
    Bluestem
flowers white against the setting sun, exhaling in a throe,
    sizzling the
memory of winter, burrowing in fallow ground, dirt deep
    in milo fields.

Sheaves of wheat grow sun yellow amid red barns, their
    doors open
in heaving sighs. Dry seedlings sprout. Corn greens on
    husks, their amber
tassels trembling in Springtime's freshening breezes.
    Amid the whistle

of swallow and sparrow, kingbird and warbler, the chug
    of tractors
scythe to plough furrows in pied daisies, uplifting the land
    from
its winter knell. The sky is blue and shaded with powder
    whiffs,

cloud shadows lazy upon the curvature of the earth.
    Hawks wheel,
their chests white against the cirrus striations, white as

hope from a once dark

world. I've become the plains, their hillocks a maze of
marvel, charmed

by the distance of distance. I've become Spring, as wind
weaves
through a lone cottonwood's quiet leaves, the nearest
sounds
a windmill's whisper, a cow's lowing call to romance.

Planting

He did what he'd always done
what dad and granddad and lord
only knows before him had done
to tame land that wouldn't be tamed
but still you had to try kids got to be fed
so after the last spring frost later
this year than ever the damned ice
coming into May he took his team
mismatched a draft named daisy
cuz he liked the sound a mule
no name didn't deserve one
strapped the harness around
his shoulder shouted a haww and
watched the plow blade slice into
black land the harness biting into
his back and thought of a future
early fall cooler days beyond summer
fence posts repaired beans and
beets canned and kept in the cellar
and he thought of planting like the
future could be tamed any more than the land

Sunset Diorama

In late August, within
the prairie between Lubbock

and Amarillo, when sunset
strokes the wheat shafts like

banjo notes, each wave flutter
glimmering as weak

starshine in gray dusk,
I hold dad's hand

as we walk the land,
our feet marking progress

like notes on a staff,
his step bass to my treble,

and he hums Mozart's
"Marche funèbre" in the deep

rumble of thunder or quotes
Shakespeare. He stops and wipes

his brow with a stained chambray sleeve,
torn from the morning's reaping.

He looks left at a herd of heifers,
each cow staring like a Greek chorus,

their lowing a soundtrack to his soliloquy.
I see his amber eyes go pale as raw flax seed

broken from tallgrass, our world a stage,
his exit cachectic, he as fragile

as the bluestem at our feet drying
into airlessness in the summer heat.

September in the Dakotas

I can't throw no more snow
it's heavy with wet and up to my knees
plus my toes gone numb and spit
damn near frozen on my lips split
I'm blind with white and here it is only
late September a cold spell shrieking in
from Canada I won't incur sin from this
cold-hearted neighbor so says Leviticus
but what's the real winter gonna be come
February or March 7 more months of misery
they say this here weather makes a man strong
we got iron in our guts up north they say
but my back's bent and my hands raw
and I don't feel like iron I feel like a mule
misused and harness broke
I can't throw no more snow

Still

The street was still
dead winds flag dropped
leaves waiting
windmill blades beyond
the streets intimating
water to be drawn
parked cars metal pinging
in the heat wooden posts
defining the street's cafe
barbershop feed and tack store
creaking groans
a lop-eared mutt the color of
last spring's mud dozing in fits
its tail disturbing flies
their movement quick to settle
all awaiting a breeze
some hope

Winter as Self Portrait

As Winter. Upper Midwest, between Mandan
and Sioux City, along the snow-mound
Missouri, the sun, eclipse black, has inhaled

in a sigh, and the memory of summer cowers
with hopelessness. Night owls swoop in hooted harm,
shunning daytime's noises, white against the gray clouds,

commas punctuating the sky in hushed murmurs,
blank verse without verbs. Eagles glide the daytime's gray.
Stoneflies, escaping ice breaks, swarm as thick as motes,

as feverish as mad dreams, hissing as falsetto organ peal.
My chest heaves, the air heavy with cold, breath pluming
in drifting want. I've become the Winter's chill.

I've become pensive December. My mouth tastes
of blood from lips cracked. I question submerging
beneath the ice-hard river, beneath the Winter loss.

Beneath the soil but still, lamentations on aging

In the emptiness of a dry season
when wind creaks through brittle
leaves beneath the creased soil more
sand than silt always seeds of passion
warm and wait as fingers probe as palms
caress.

Spring rains have ceased. Summer heat has withered.
Fall grayness suffocates to numbness. Yet despite
yet even through yet a current flows subterranean
like memory and waits as fingers probe as palms
caress.

The winter tree is bent with pods pale around the
trunk laid bare under a darkening sky under skyless clouds.
In the stillness of a late season, roots still dig deep
through clay for love's wetness as fingers probe as palms
caress.

There's desiccation in the flesh as leaves fall and blow
across the brown ground. But leaves pirouette in dance
and chime on ice dreaming to rise and reunite with trees
in spring green renewed as fingers probe and palms
caress.

In seasons after seasons

your touch constant your warmth
the small of your back small your
tongue on my teeth your lips
soft on my lips your body May
not June September not March
you in my arms cool after cold
breezes after burn in dry summers
your spring following winter's chill
I with you in you of you ever for you
in seasons after seasons loving you

Alone Together

Act 1 Some Guy

The Hole, Houston coffee house, folk music venue, underground, private, personal, pure escape. I'd go there, 1964, my pre-hippie days, maybe before I even knew what a hippie was, but I was sure on the path to hippiedom, trying to be cool, or at least out there, somewhere, remote, aloof, odd. I'd walk to The Hole and smell the java, as deep dark as an orc's home in a primeval forest, the underbrush dense with my caffeinated dreams. I'd hear the music drifting from the door like a mystic's incantation, enticing me to solace.

"How many?" The hostess at the door asked, her hair plaited and dangling over her left shoulder, her right cheek decorated with a hand-painted sunflower, she standing there in her mini dress, all legs and allure. I was in love.

"One, just me," of course, alone, again. "Unless you'd like to spend the rest of your life with me," I said with what I hoped was a cool, new, never-heard-before come on.

Act 2 Shirl

I hate this place. Dreary music, too much smoke in the air, coffee fumes, yuck. And loner losers. That's all we ever get in The Hole, dud dudes who listen to downer music, folk songs about depression, though I do dig Dylan's "The Lonesome Death of Hattie Carroll" and, man, to hear Townes Van Zandt singing "Marie," well

God damn. When he croons with that Marlboro voice all soaked in bourbon, saying, "maybe me and Marie could find a burned out van and do a little settlin' down," that hits you man. You can feel his pain. I'd get it on with him, but he's always in some kind of world all to himself up there on the stage, the smoke from his ciggie swirling around his head like a curtain, him alone in a fog, part smoke, part dope, part isolato. Still, one kickin' dude. I hope he makes it big in the business. Still, I can't believe I left South Texas for this, standing in the heat, my hands holding lukewarm wishes.

Act 3 Townes

"Hey Bob, you got a D string? I damn busted mine, and I'm 'bout to go on in 5 minutes."

"Sure 'nough Townes," he said, reaching into his guitar case. "Take this," so I did, spooled the string through the 4 hole, tightened it a few twists, and asked Bob to give me a low E to tune.

"Alrighty Dighty. I'm set. Thanks my man," and I shined my Nocona boots on the back of my jeans, tilted my Stetson down low on my head, and hit the stage, looking left to see if Shirl was still at the door.

Applause

"Howdy, brothers and sisters. Great seeing you tonight. I brought my best friend," I said, patting my guitar on its pick guard, "'cuz I sure as hell got no one else."

Polite laughter

"Any requests," I asked, hoping no one would suggest a song.

"Can you play your Shrimp song, dude?"

Oh no, not him again. The same lame guy who comes here every week, sitting by himself over by the dying Ficus tree. Always asks me to sing the dumbest song I ever wrote.

"You got it my man," and I set off, strumming my chords, hearing myself sing, "Goodbye mama shrimp, papa shake my hand. Here comes the shrimper for to take me to Louisian.'" And the crowd howls, no telling why, 'cuz, come on, it's a song about some poor baby shrimp getting caught and heading for the shrimp boil. Damn, poor little sucker, all alone in the turgid surf of the Gulf of Mexico.

Epilogue The Hole

It sagged a bit. That's what you get when a roof leaks and pipes burst from time to time, streaming green gunk down the walls like lichen on the dark sides of dying trees.

The Hole was north of Westheimer, south of Montrose, brownstones lined like tombstones, like shark's teeth, like druid's talons stained in blood. Pitiful trees fought for life in cobbled streets, each tree getting at least 2 feet of dirt to struggle in.

To the left of The Hole was an empty lot, strangling weeds growing next to broken bottles and used syringes. To the right was a dilapidated flop house for hobos and has-beens, most of the second-floor windows broken out, a few light bulbs flickering dimly, dots and dashes for hope.

People lined up outside The Hole, individuals, no two some lovers, no groups of groupies, loners seeking music to steal their souls.

Chapter 3: Love and Loss

Love Sounds Like

Love sounds   like the sky   beyond thought
in my chest as through my fingertips synapses exploding
into lightning   along piano keys   the quiet hum
of a tuning fork thrum reverberating and echoing
   birdsongs

Water to root, sun to stem

as water to root
sun to stem, you rise
outward toward growth

your sun radiates
uplifting as geese in flight
defining contours

gray aloft the earth
undulating bright
allowing me

to break through compacted
sod and concrete barriers
water and sun raised

Breathless

Caravaggio called it chiaroscuro,
where darkness disappears from the light,
like the Chichauhaun sun
setting at night,
light illuminating beauty,
shadows creating mystery.
That's you, leaning against
the door to our yard,
your left shoulder raised toward
the pasture, light caressing,
your right shoulder leaning into suspense.
I'm behind you, enthralled
by each curve, dip and mound,
you, the landscape of our farm,
cleft and sculptured swirl,
the swirl of your hair bound in a braid,
your body aglow as if daubed
by a painterly hand, beguiled
brushstrokes tracing your contours.
Dusk colors of sunset
becoming evening warm you
in embrace. And you start to turn,
the tug of your chin inching,
a stray tendril from your upswept
hair enticing, and I await your splendor,
breathless in the desert.

Only geese fly straight lines

The wheel ruts scribed the prairie snow like meridians on traveler's maps, pathways evolving from now to next, lines curving in impromptu plans.

"Where to?" he asked, eyeing the sky as if clouds told tales with trusting advice.

"Try right," she answered. "I always veer toward the shadows," earth askew, trees shedding leaves in winter chill, branches bending above the pond, western shorelines pushed randomly by contrary winds.

"You think it's there?" he asked again.

She breathed in deeply, held a sigh like a wish, then weaving her arm in his, said, "Let's try."

Posted

he'd sent the postcard she said
her head held low in her hands
her knuckles white her eyes red
right before shipping out
to the Middle East he wrote
posted to who knows wherever
Anbar is tell you more later babe gotta go
we're climbing in our C-17 transport
from Naval Base San Diego
me and my squad taking off over the
ocean the sun reflecting like an invitation
my sarge joked more like hazard lights
to me but what do I know a grunt coming
from nowhere Silent Knife, Oklahoma
biggest body of water I'd seen that pond
in your grandpa's back 40 I can see our
lighthouse we visited up on the hill
overlooking Point Loma that day you wore
blue gingham the color of your eyes
the color of the Pacific at dawn the day
I asked you for your hand me kneeling
like some damned picture show star
you laughing a smudge of lipstick on your
teeth you my girl then and now and forever
the card arrived almost a year to the day
after he was reported KIA delayed by
bureaucracy postmarked dead letter Wash DC
she kept the postcard on the fridge
pinned like a bug in biology class
and read his last line see you soon hon
the words thumbed and fading

The Red Bentwood Painted by Pipe Smoke

It's the smoke I remember, tendrils rising,
drawn into the thin Winter heat
like creeper vines from Grandpa's pipe,
held in his right hand, as he leaned back
in his red Bentwood rocker.

The smoke, sweet and woodsy,
his own special blend of cherry
and Missouri burley, wove between
the oaks and cottonwoods warming
our farmstead like generations of family.

He sat in the chair,
ringed by an embrace of wild foliage
that no one had planted, that no one tended,
and he looked toward rain clouds
building above the train trestle

banked behind our barn, the trains
running every hour like geese flying south.
The smoke from his pipe hung
on his tweed jacket like a pocket square,
hung in the air like memory.

Now, I smell his pipe smoke when I ride
the city highways, when I enter my office
at the school, when I walk around his farm,
my hand trailing through the wispy tops
of the Winter wheat. Even now,

when I visit his land on those rare weekends,
the kids and I, and hear the whirr of crickets
like the sound of trains rattling over tracks,
I remember the smell of his pipe smoke
and see him leaning back in his red Bentwood rocker.

Love/Loveless

Act 1. You and me

Grilled salmon perfectly browned in warm butter beside a quartered lemon slice on two Wedgewood plates. A carrot-sculpted rosette. Two glasses of rosé. Brown, yellow, blue, orange, red passion. "We'll both have the salmon." The server left us alone to hold hands in the flickering light of a candle, the shape of light caressing your face like breezes rustling a redbird's feathers.

Act 2. Her

I just want someone. Why can't I find someone? They come in here every week, sit at the same table, order the same fresh-frozen salmon, in Omaha, hold hands, never see me, see only each other, like I'm a distant noise, a car crash in some other neighborhood, a solar flare whose eruption won't affect their climate-controlled environment, a damned iceberg calving, dissolving into the sea, disappearing into atoms small enough to be carried on the waves of their love sighs.

Act 3. Me

You caulk the seams between my stone edges and your seamlessness. You are chocolate drizzled on my finger to lick. Let my thumb inscribe circles on your palm to plot roads we'll travel. Let my tongue touch your tongue and speak of time and song.

Act 4. You

You help me see light in different colors. The other men I've known have been as cataract, their needs obscuring my vision of self. "Come on, babe, just this once, I promise." "Hey, get me a beer, won't ya'," he'd say while scratching his lazy ass." "Let me tell you what I think." "That chick friend of yours has a big mouth, always goin' on about her this or that. I mean, who gives a you know what?!" You listen. You take the words I speak and weave them into garlands.

Act 5. Her

Four more hours of this shift. Burning my hands on hot plates, my soul searing in loss. Then what? An empty night of Hulu. Bottles of bud diesel clanking against my teeth, the sound resounding throughout my hollow apartment. Endless loops of "Beautiful Pain," Eminem screeching in AK-47 staccatos, "Yesterday was the tornado warning/ Today's like the morning after/Your world is torn in half/. . . It's like an enormous asthma."

Those two, sitting at the table, eyes fondling each other, their hands linked like a bridge joining his hemisphere to hers.

I'm falling, my gravity gone and I'm reeling into ether, nothing tethering me. Loveless. I want. And my want echoes.

A Truck in Snow

He parked the truck beneath the oak behind the barn across the lake then handed the keys to his younger brother Hank with a backslap and wink, walked to her and said, "Don't worry, Beth, I'll be fine, you know me, always careful," and hugged her, kissed her, and turned toward the road, a bus waiting.

2004, spring, the oaks in bud, starting to leaf out. He was off to Iraq, they said, but who ever really knows. Once on the bus, he waved to the family through fly-speck windows, they waving back, and he was gone, dust pluming on the country road. Beth wrote daily, at first, and waited.

No news, but the family said, "he's busy, probably, girl. He'll write when he gets a chance," and spring became summer. The truck sat beneath the oak, baking in the Kansas heat, the sun radiating off the truck's red panels, the truck's hood pinging in the heat, like a heart beating.

She wrote weekly, her time taken up with chores, and she waited, and she was pregnant. No news,

but the local paper reported heavy fighting near Al Anbar, where he was maybe stationed, so the family said, "stay calm, Beth. He's involved. He'll be fine. You know him, always takes care." In autumn, the leaves fell, littering the truck with pastels, leaves stuck to the truck's windows like lost letters. Beth wrote weekly, mostly, but sometimes a month would go by.

No news, and she was 5 months and showing. The house was heavy with quiet. No one in the family talked about the war, anymore. When winter hit, snow covered the truck, covered the oaks, covered the barn, iced the lake, and the farm was iced in fear, like nighttime chills.

The baby was born after that first snow, a boy they named after him, his father gone to war. Another truck stopped by the house later that winter, and a man got out. He tugged down his khaki dress uniform jacket, straightened his tie and hat, and looked toward the house with downcast eyes, eyes that were tired from telling tales before. He plodded through the snow with heavy boots. Before he knocked on the door, Beth opened it, the baby on her hip, her eyes starting to redden like his truck in the snow, buried in cold.

News had finally arrived.

Cottonwood

I'm lost.

The prairie grass whistling moans
In the high winds from the foothills
Rushing through the flatlands
Rushing through me like images
Of you leaving.

I'm lost.

Our home empty
Only calendar pages lined through
Days removed our past excised
Pages littering the floor
Our life's detritus.

I'm lost.

You were as cottonwood
Roots seeking deep water
Roots foraging through hard clay
My density my rock strewn
My windblown desiccation

You're gone.

the echo between passing hills

Me

Why can't I have time in your space? Why must I stand outside looking in through frosted glass? You enter me. Greedily. Devouring. Taking. I reach, but your air ices.

You

It's a whirr. A sound that I swat away like mosquitoes hissing. A chilled breeze. An apparition without form.

Me

My ribs are cracking in your vacuum. This want feels skeletal, slithering through me like lichen, sun starved. Where is your warmth? Touch? Why does this always happen,to me. Connections that fray like severed synapses. Electricity that sizzles then deadens, narcotized?

You

What does this person want? Always. Clinging. Cloying. Clawing. You're cacti, and my skin is a rash. No. Not cacti. Too assertive. You're a pale rose, six days past the sell-by-date, blackening.

Prophesies

We'd sit in the diner for Sunday suppers, surrounded by grease fire and bellowed orders for fried chicken and giblet gravy. Grandpa held court at the head of our table, like Ezekiel, prophesizing about exile. "I've seen it all, boys, and it ain't pretty, believe me All Mighty, but we got us some hope, I tell you," crossing his heart, him in his rolled-up dress shirt, starched as stiff as the gospel, as holey as Palm Sunday.

With his dinner fork held aloft as a scepter, he'd preach forgiveness from Colossians 3:13, saying in hushed tones over his grits, "Bear with each other, boys, and forgive one another, even if you've got some damned grievance, ya hear?"

Or he'd lash out at sinners (forgetting all about forgiveness, I guess). "You remember your Psalms, like 145:20, where the Lord says He'll destroy them wicked ones," and gramps would wipe the waffle syrup off his whiskers.

I'd see travelers in the diner come and go like calendar pages turning, like pilgrims to a shrine. They'd nurse a cup of dime coffee, their heads bowed over the black steam, the steam clouding their dreams deferred, and wear work clothes brown from the land's dirt, as brown as the grease-fire that hung in the air, brown as a sepia photo in a family's discarded album.

Their eyes pooled in their coffee cup's reflection, the diner's harsh light against the night's darkness, their moment of rest in a worn booth, plastic seats torn like a map, each crack a destination sought, a path missed. They might have sought Jeremiah's "good way" and "rest for their souls," but I never saw any rest in their restlessness, their alcohol-stewed disturbance, eyes red.

The diner's gone, shuttered soon after grandpa died, when an overpass was constructed so people could get someplace else, other pilgrims seeking a new gospel. And dust settled on the prophesies of my youth.

Pale green and garnet

Her dress once green
now pale as milkweed
washed daily worn daily
to threadbare no money
she lived in his Bismarck
rental while he worked
the oil fields in Williston
she wondered if he'd get
a strike wondered if he'd
come back flush wondered
if he'd come back at all
hoping he wouldn't
as she touched the welt
beneath her eye her eye cried
red as red as the glass garnet
promise ring he'd given her
the one he called a ruby jewel

The life of Grandpa's House

I walked across his bedroom floor
each creak the whine of timeworn wood
and stepped through his days from youth to age
I saw him when he played sandlot ball
his hands big in those Ty Cobb mitts
or toted my mom in her sleepless turns
she on his shoulder through bat-flight nights
I saw him bent over bills stacked high
a pencil nub marking digits denied
then watched him fret when her curfew passed
him fearing some boy's drunken drive
on ice storm glazed or lightning struck streets
next walking her toward a canopy
set up in the house for her bridal day
his feet scuffed the floor in stumbling steps
until I came along his first grandson
and in the house playing hide and seek
now he's lying in his bed bricks lifting the head
to help drain his phlegm and clear his lungs
a life of smoking unfiltered drags
a life bent under the family's care
I'm standing beside him a soothing touch
a wisp of gray a lock misplaced
my feet pained as the floorboards creak

This Year Darkening

I feel it, this year, as a bird fleeing
with mottled wings from a songless cage.
This year, I feel it, bone cells dying,
necroptosis serrating to amputate.

I see it, this year, words undulating,
hazed as gnawing worms on a writhing page.
This year, I see it, rough boughs of shaking
trees, limbs bowing from age's pillage.

I hear it, this year, a white wind whining
in moans, groans of life's fading umbrage.
This year, I hear it, a faint song singing
of love loss, of life losing, disengaged.

I know it, my rusting clock unwinding
this year, my darkening shroud awaiting.

Ice Shattering

Sam

I had known her/loved her/or at least really liked her in high school then I went my way she went her way the way that people separate like chaff from wheat when winds drift like surf from sand when tides surge so I didn't think about her (much) and I bet if I crossed the threshold of her mind it was like dust at the door or a snowflake melting (hissss) on her windowsill but when I saw her again at the coffee shop where I worked as a barista $14 an hour making steamed this or foamed that she looked awesome not having aged a bit vs. me with my balding pate she wearing what looked like a Dolce or a Prada or a Moschino how would I know me wearing a goofy barista's uniform with my name tag but I knew it was her so I said, "Jill!" and she looked through me toward the menu board, so I tried again "Jill, it's me, Sam . . . remember?" and her eyes glazed over me like an iceberg and I shivered calving into the frozen sea of my lost youth my present freezer burned by her chilled emotion

Jill

"I'll have a large frozen macchiato half caf half decaf no whip no caramel drizzle low fat little ice heavy on the foam" how's this guy know my name? Stan? Is that what he said? Don't know him don't want to know him yuck some loser dude working at the Target coffee stop "oh and put the macchiato in two plastic cups I don't like to get my hands too cold don't want these pinkies to be frozen"

Jason said we'd meet his parents tonight George and Donna so I've got to be chill do my good girl act can't lose this one he's got bu-ku moola with his fancy killer Jag those designer clothes maybe I'll wear my old lady gray Talbot's business suit and mary jane black pumps (dorky) oh yeh and my pearls that grandma gave me back in middle school that I never wore never thought I'd have to ha my besties them bitches would laugh their asses off on that

Jason

"OK hon, pick you up at 7:00 kisses" I'm so excited gonna show off my girl to the parents they'll love love love her I mean she's just what they've always wanted classy super sweet like frosting on a cake and kind and caring and you know just real I've never heard her say one bad thing about anyone she's a keeper believe me she'd never cold shoulder anyone too kind for that

Wrought Things

Try if you can to see the sky,
blue for those even happy at night,
but plight and strife darken life.
Terrors tame light creating things wrought,

and shall and will become sodden sighs
when realizing that try but cannot denies.
The road seemingly straight dips and dies
descending into troubling things wrought.

Or suffer an esophageal probe
to find the source of your wayward soul.
What lies within the twists and folds,
the mangled morass of things wrought--

skin, breath, psychic mold?
Destructive coughs, destructive thoughts?
You're delving to find the exit toll,
with blighted sight lost in things wrought.

Personal, political, spiritual, climatical
knot in tangles of intestinal coils
that burst like shotgunned birds from flight.
Sun-leaping happy men, their waxed wings
melting, plummet from sky in things wrought.

The Silence

She stood at the window, lace drapes
half drawn, the sky darkening at dusk,
darkening under sullen skies, the sun

setting behind the gray hills rising like
doubt beyond the blackening snow,
geese ellipses against the clouds.

A bluebottle fly hushed against her screen,
hail torn. Her men had gone, the boys off
to cities for jobs away from the land,

streets replacing silos, to carry briefcases
instead of hauling hay, Joe, her husband
of 43 years, heart-stopped dead, his eyes

as empty as the plains surrounding their farm.
"Now what?" she asked the silence
seeping into her home like chilled air.

Sepia

They had a barn, pride of possession, poets of old called it *mimesis,* so my whiskey-soured professor said, when wood and fields reflected their green life, reflected his love for her. Their barn was nailed tight at right angles, the beams planed straight, hinges oiled, hay raked. The barn rested in a tended field, spring-alive from the windmill's well water clear and deep. Apple trees in their orchard bloomed fulsome. And he tended the barn and land lovingly, thinking of her with each nail hammered, each scythe swept, each apple plucked and polished, under pink skies where even clouds promised the scent of rain. And he whistled Willie Nelson's "Always on My Mind." He could see her in the farmhouse window.

Then stage four arrived like an in-law, a counselor's note sent home to reprimand, and she was gone, in weeks, her breathing the rasp of filed metal.

In time the barn's beams swayed in decay, his attentions distant, his eyes vacant. Doors hung askew on rusted bolts, stalls echoed as empty as wormed wood, and mice entered sibilant, filling his void with mischief, their scurrying feet the chatter of thrown bones. The windmill shattered, lightning struck, its blades airless in the farm's dead breeze, and the field's grasses dried like barbed wire, cicadas screaming in the summer heat.

One dusk, he drank boiled coffee, more dregs than beans, left fried eggs to dry ochre on ignored plates, and packed his truck: their bedspring with splines spent, a bentwood rocker, its wicker seats unraveling, and his Martin guitar, strings sprung, sound hole stuffed with calendar clippings of lost birthdays and anniversaries.

He turned the truck onto a rutted road, dusty with a past harvest's wheat chaff, and left his life, once green, now the color of sunset under cloud-worried skies, the color of sepia.

Them

1. Her

The seams of her silk pants edged sharply as a tightened
    garrote.

Her latte eyes, the color of skylines under cloud cover,
    revealed nothing.

All façade. Within her bones rubbed raw, her blood
    jumped brambles like rabbits fleeing foxes.

He had done this to her, casting a shadow
like barbed spines of leafless trees
on frozen days.

2. Him

He gulped coffee, his veins caffeine-trembling like seismic
    shifts. His suitcase was half filled: their baby's tattered
    bear, one eye missing;

a box of seashell shards, gathered before she shared
    the news;

a torn wedding photo, her eyes shining like Winter ice.

He planned to finish packing
before she returned.

Then he'd leave.

After Thought

after wind shears
after angry clouds

serrate like knife edges
after cottonwood shed seeds

like lost children
after winds sting with memory

like shrieking raptors
after fears lace in tallgrass nettles

and strangle
after flint steps break

into contempt
and blood seeps into sand

after tornadoes whirl thought thoughtlessly
like I've thought words onto you

each word a glass sliver under skin
after you asked why

and I answered
with a twister's dead eye

after sorrow like rainfall
and skies blackening

I walk toward distant horizons
darkening on my bitten tongue

Meditations on Bee Watching

I want to hover.

I've turned left and right, left and right.
I've sipped and stopped and stooped
and stayed stymied by this or that
and sought solutions from
exhausting options, the tumbledown

result of a world vibrating, a
carnival house of mirrors reflecting
reflections of reflections, a
constellation of metroplex overpasses,
cars swarming, their night lights a maze

of mayhem. Daily mass murders.
Weekly invective from elected officials.
Miscommunicated missives from 24/7
newscasts. I'm swirling in mind mists,
a fugue of feverish hysteria. Noise.

There's a carpenter bee outside
my window, hovering, though the wind
is rolling swollen, though enticing
flowers beckon through thorned delight,
though rain shears its tiffany wings.

Bereft of honied dreams, hiveless
solitary, the bee whirrs into silence
its stable flight, its focused task,

not to build intricacies but wood-
gnawn holes of absence.

I want its drone to drown the noise,
its static flight within what roils,
air without deceitful dissent, without
polemical sting, direction driven only
by the anesthesia of numb hums.

I want to hover.

nothing

Every day. For the last month. Or more. I've lost track.
The days like blown sand in a dry month. I've sat on the
hard bench outside our house. Enjoying the bench's pain.
Like penance. The wooden slats digging into me. Raking
as peregrine talons. Each day is gray. To me. I feel the gray
shadow heavy in the gray sky. Black clouds smothering the
sun. And I slump into the wooden bench weather torn. I
feel myself drawn beneath the heavy skies. Breathing in
tornado screams. And think of the last time I saw you.
Walking away.

Sunshine enters like a hesitant guest

I'm alone in the room's darkness.
Sunshine enters through the east window

like a hesitant guest, but shadows still hold
me bowed, behind me in doubt, in want, in need.

It's hard to forget what's been said . . . or
which words I never stated.

Where are they now, my family from once?
Dan's gone, of course, disease reclaiming

the past, his cancer a needle's prick in my
love, a scar that won't heal, now bandaged

on my arm like old age scabbing, failing to heal.
The kids are displaced, Dan Jr., wife Molly, and his family

to Chicago, Sue Beth and her son (her husband
disclaimed, barely a mote sifting in stale air) to Seattle.

They write, now and sometimes, maybe Christmas
    or Thanksgiving
("Hi Mom. How's the farm? Abilene still hot in September?

Still cold in May?"). No one visits. ("It's so far, Mom,
    especially with no
direct flights to Kansas." "We're pretty busy with our jobs,
    you know."

"Money's kind of tight right now." "Molly's still peeved
    at what you said.")
Mostly, the house is quiet, except for crows cawing
    blackness in the fields

and my sewing machine whirring like mice nibbling
    memories in dark corners.
I could make little Georgie a cap for Seattle's winter.
    I could sew Mary

a white blouse for her confirmation.   Though I don't
    have their addresses.
The clothing would sit on my bedstand with other
    loose threads.

Dr. Steven M. Gerson, Professor Emeritus, Johnson County Community College, was named 2003-2004 Kansas Professor of the Year, chosen by the Carnegie Foundation. He is the co-author, along with his wife Sharon Gerson, of 13 college-level textbooks and the author of three poetry chapbooks: *Once Planed Straight: Poetry of the Prairies; Viral: Love and Losses in the Time of Insanity; and The 13th Floor: Step into Anxiety* (Spartan Press-KC). He has published over 300 poems in many journals and was named a finalist twice for the North Dakota State University Press Poetry of the Plains and Prairies award. Steve is most proud of his 50+ year marriage to Sharon, for whom all his love poems are written, his wonderful family of Stacy, Stefani, and Rob, and for the joy of spending time with his three grandchildren: Sophia, Samantha, and Jacob. These people are the poetry of Steve's life.

This project was made possible, in part, by generous support from the Osage Arts Community.

Osage Arts Community provides temporary time, space and support for the creation of new artistic works in a retreat format, serving creative people of all kinds — visual artists, composers, poets, fiction and nonfiction writers. Located on a 152-acre farm in an isolated rural mountainside setting in Central Missouri and bordered by ¾ of a mile of the Gasconade River, OAC provides residencies to those working alone, as well as welcoming collaborative teams, offering living space and workspace in a country environment to emerging and mid-career artists. For more information, visit us at www.osageac.org

Osage Arts Community

www.ingramcontent.com/pod-product-compliance
Lightning Source LLC
Chambersburg PA
CBHW031243120626
46545CB00007B/2625

9 781958 182550

"Steve Gerson delivers brilliantly etched vignettes of America's psyche, soul, and temperament in his fourth collection of lyrical poetry and poetic prose. Once more, in unsurpassed fashion, he captures the essence of the nation's too little remembered, easily forgotten, readily ignored, continuously ignored heartland. His elegant writings touch on abuse and enduring love, shattered hopes and dashed expectations, stunted dreams and steely determination to weather the storm, both literally and otherwise. But even Gerson's darkest representations are, happily, leavened by the beauty of their delivery—which includes wonderfully apt titles--stitched together in seamless fashion with a fluidity seldom attained by other chroniclers of Americana. One fortunate enough to devour Gerson's written words experiences a multitude of emotions, ranging from anguish and remembrance to hopefulness and sheer delight. More than matching his earlier rich offerings, *And the Land Dreams Darkly* further cements Steve Gerson's standing as a leading 21st century poet-artist. Its creative entries skillfully explore a fitting arc of yearnings, life transformations, and, in characteristic fashion for the author, love and loss."

-Dr. Robert C. Cottrell, *The Year Without a World Series: Major League Baseball and the Road to the 1994 Players' Strike.*

"Steve's poetry and short stories make you think, make you feel, make you despair, and make you hope. Steve's vignettes bring each character and the places they inhabit to life in the span of a few words or phrases, fully realized in your mind's eye. His evocative writing creates snapshots of human existence, spanning all its highs and lows. From the humble and downtrodden, to those hopefully in love, and to those despondent in the face of their loss, Steve carries you through on a wave of emotion. His writing makes you think about your own place in the world."

-Stacy Harken, JD, Information Architect/Technical Writer, Garmin Industries

"Steve Gerson's latest collection *And the Land Dreams Darkly* is his best to date. In this offering from Spartan Press, Gerson plays with genre from Japanese form poetry to micro plays, narrative poetry to short-short fiction. Most memorable are the sensory snapshots in time like the scene in 'The Moment' where kids are drinking cider and hoping Jim might play the fiddle. Or the creak in the floor from 'The Life of Grandpa's House.' Readers are won over by the characters who are 'planting in dry land' and 'charting a life' across the middle section of the country. This collection is for anyone who would like to sit with someone else's experience for a while."

-Dr. Beth Gulley, English professor, author of *Dragon Eggs* and *Frog Joy*.

"'Followed sometimes by you just never know.'" "'Cleaning our past for the future.'" "'In seasons after seasons.'" "'Now what?'" Gerson captures the raw reality of life—the good, the bad, the expected, and the surprising. The moments found in his poetry resonate. You can feel the experiences through his intentional words. Like lyrics in a song, and visuals in a movie, the words tell a story. Gerson's stories are woven throughout the occurrences that happen in life—to your friend, to your parents, to your neighbors, or to yourself. Though the poems stand alone in vignettes, as the reader, you are captured, wanting to know what happens next.

-Dr. Stefani Buchwitz, Director, Self Graduate Programs, University of Kansas